the g.i. diet

GUIDE TO SHOPPING AND EATING OUT

RICK GALLOP

Past President of the Heart & Stroke Foundation of Ontario

RANDOM HOUSE CANADA

National Library of Canada Cataloguing in Publication

Gallop, Rick
The G.I. diet guide to shopping and eating out / Rick Gallop.

Includes index.
ISBN 0-679-31391-5

1. Glycemic index.   2. Reducing diets.   I. Title.
RM222.2.G3425 2005   613.2'5   C2004-907109-2

Printed and bound in Canada

Visit Random House of Canada Limited's website:
www.randomhouse.ca

Contents

Introduction

Congratulations! The fact that you're reading this means you've decided to go on the G.I. Diet—the easiest, healthiest, most effective route to permanent weight loss. Whether you've been losing weight on the plan for a while or are just about to embark on it, *The G.I. Diet Guide to Shopping and Eating Out* will not only make following the program easier, but will show you how much fun you can have while losing weight. Being on the G.I. Diet doesn't mean you have to radically change your lifestyle. It was designed with the real world in mind so that you can dine out, travel, celebrate special events, snack and still lose those extra unwanted pounds. No matter where you go or what the occasion, there are always delicious green-light options to enjoy, and the purpose of this book is to list them for you. It's intended to be a complementary tool with *The G.I. Diet* and/or *Living the G.I. Diet,* and not a replacement for either of those two books, since it doesn't explain the principles of the diet or how it works. Rather it's to be carried and consulted on your weekly grocery trip, as you grab a bite on the run or when you're out with friends at your favourite restaurant.

This book is divided into two main sections. Part One, "At the Grocery Store," takes you aisle by aisle through the supermarket. While the food guides in *The G.I. Diet* and *Living the G.I. Diet* are organized by meal or food group, this guide is organized the way a typical grocery store is, starting with the produce section and ending with frozen foods. You can start at the beginning and let the book navigate your shopping cart through the supermarket aisles, or you can look up a specific food in the index, which starts on page 84.

Part Two, "Eating Out," lists the green-light options available at a number of popular fast food chains and also gives some helpful guidelines to follow while dining out. It lists the dishes you'd typically find at Italian, Greek, Chinese, Indian,

Mexican, Thai and Japanese restaurants and points out the green-light options. Eating out should be a fun social occasion and this guide will help you enjoy it without worrying about your waistline.

One of the most popular features of the G.I. Diet is that you don't have to count calories, add points or measure carbs in order to follow it. I've been researching glycemic ratings, fat and calorie levels, and ingredient lists of food products and menu items, and have done all the math for you. Now all you have to do is look at the colour-coded charts to find out which foods you can fill your shopping cart with or order in a restaurant. Although I've included the red- and yellow-light columns along with the green-light, this book is really about the green-light, about all the foods you can enjoy while slimming down. This diet isn't about deprivation and going hungry, it's about making the right choices and eating until you're satisfied. Food is one of life's greatest pleasures and you can definitely indulge in it. Enjoy!

As always, your feedback is extremely valuable. I can be reached through my website, at **www.gidiet.com.**

PART ONE

At the Grocery Store

Following the G.I. Diet really begins once you clear out your pantry and refrigerator of red-light products and make a trip to the grocery store to stock up on green-light ones. A word of advice: don't go to the supermarket until after you've eaten a meal. One of the worst mistakes you can make is to go grocery shopping on an empty stomach—you'll only feel tempted by all those red-light ready-to-eat foods. You may also want to do a bit of planning before you go. Check out the recipe sections in *The G.I. Diet* and *Living the G.I. Diet,* choose a few that appeal to you and make a list of the ingredients you'll need. Then take it and this guide along with you to the store. With these tools in hand, you'll find it easy to load your cart with delicious food, and I hope you'll be introduced to some new favourites.

How to Use this Guide

I've organized the food in this guide the way you would typically find it in the supermarket, in sections such as the Produce Aisle, the Deli Counter, the Bakery, the Meat Counter, the Beverage Aisle, the Frozen Food Section and so on. Within each of these sections, you'll find categories of food such as vegetables, processed meat, breads, etc. All are listed in one of the three traffic-light-based colour columns.

If you find a food in the red-light column that you would normally add to your shopping cart, look at what's listed beside it in the green-light column. There is almost always a wonderful green-light alternative to a red- or yellow-light food. If, for example, you would normally buy a cantaloupe, which is a red-light food, choose some peaches or oranges or grapes, or any of the other green-light choices instead. Remember that if you want to look up a specific food rather than a whole category, you can look at the index on pages 84–92.

I've generally tried to stay away from listing specific brands. There are just far too many out there and they vary from region to region. For the most part they don't have any bearing on the G.I. rating of a particular food anyway. For example, 1% cottage cheese or whole wheat spaghetti or Dijon mustard is pretty much the same no matter who's made it. The only times I have mentioned brands is when it does make a difference. For example, most cold cereals are red light, but Kashi Go Lean is a green-light product.

It can be a bit tricky sometimes trying to distinguish the green-light products from the red-light. Take bread for example. We know that white bread is red light, since it spikes glucose levels in your bloodstream, releasing insulin, which stores the glucose as fat. The green-light alternative is whole-grain bread, but many of the healthy-looking multi-grain loaves out there are not exactly what they seem. Some of them list "enriched white flour" or "unbleached flour" in the ingredient list, and this puts a red flashing light over them. The first ingredient listed on bread should always be "100% whole wheat flour" or "100% whole-grain flour." If "stone-ground" is mentioned, even better. So checking ingredient lists and labels can be important, and I'll give you some guidelines to follow.

Reading Labels

When buying a green-light food such as a loaf of whole wheat bread or a bottle of low-fat salad dressing, you'll find several kinds to choose from. How do you decide which to add to your shopping cart? Read the nutritional label on the package.

Now I know these labels aren't exactly consumer friendly, but they do contain some helpful information. Here are the seven key components that will help you make the best choice:

1. **Serving size:** Is this realistic, or is the manufacturer low-balling it so the calorie and fat content look better than the competition? When comparing one brand with another, make sure you're comparing the same serving sizes.

2. **Calories:** The product with the least amount of calories is obviously the best choice.

3. **Fat:** Choose the product with the least amount of fat, particularly saturated fat, and avoid any product that contains trans fat—the worst of the saturated fats.

4. **Protein:** The higher the protein level the better. Protein acts as a brake on the digestive system, lowering the G.I. rating of the food.

Nutrition Facts
Valeur nutritive

Serving 1 cup (55 g)
Portion de 1 tasse (55 g)

Amount Per Serving	% Daily Value
Teneur par portion	% valeur quotidienne

Calories / Calories 190	
Fat / Lipides 1.5 g	**2** %
Saturated / saturés 0 g	
+ Trans / trans 0 g	**0** %
Cholesterol / Cholestérol 0 mg	**0** %
Sodium / Sodium 90 mg	**4** %
Potassium / Potassium 500 mg	**14** %
Carbohydrate / Glucides 31 g	**10** %
Fibre / Fibres 10 g	**42** %
Sugars / Sucres 6 g	
Protein / Protéines 14 g	
Vitamin A / Vitamine A	0 %
Vitamin C / Vitamine C	0 %
Calcium / Calcium	6 %
Iron / Fer	15 %
Phosphorus / Phosphore	20 %

5. **Fibre:** The product with the higher fibre content is the best choice, whether it's soluble or insoluble. Fibre, like protein, significantly lowers the G.I. rating.

6. **Sugar:** Try to avoid products that contain added sugar. Choose the ones with sugar substitutes or none at all. "Nonfat" products that contain added sugar aren't non-fattening!

7. **Sodium (Salt):** Look for lower sodium levels. Sodium increases water retention, which causes bloating and added weight and impacts blood pressure.

TO SUM UP:
The best green-light buy is
- Lower in calories
- Lower in fat, particularly saturated fat
- Higher in fibre
- Lower in sugar and sodium

The Green-Light Grocery Guide

The Produce Aisle

Vegetables and fruit are the cornerstone of the G.I. Diet. They are low G.I. and high in fibre, nutrients, vitamins and minerals. Cooking them raises their G.I. and reduces their nutrient content, so use as little water as possible and cook only until they are crisp-tender—or try eating them raw.

Soy-based foods such as tofu are high in protein, low in saturated fat and good for a healthy heart. Many supermarkets carry something called veggie ground round, which looks and tastes exactly like ground beef, but is made of Textured Vegetable Protein (TVP). TVP is used to make veggie burgers, veggie breakfast links and other products. It's an excellent choice whether you're vegetarian or not.

You can often find nuts and dried fruit in the produce section of the supermarket. Most dried fruit is very high in sugar and therefore red light. However there are some yellow-light choices, and all dried fruit can be used in modest quantities in baking.

Nuts are an excellent source of good fats and protein, and green-light nuts contain even more monounsaturated (best) fat than the others. Remember, though, that all nuts are calorie dense and so must be eaten in limited quantities, about eight to twelve per serving. It's just too easy to unconsciously consume a whole bowl of nuts while watching television, but this quantity would equal your total calorie needs for an entire day!

VEGETABLES		
Broad Beans	Artichokes	Alfalfa sprouts
Parsnips	Beets	Arugula
Plantains	Corn	Asparagus
Potatoes (except new potatoes)	Pumpkin	Beans (green/wax)
	Squash	Belgian endive
Rutabaga	Sweet potatoes	Bell peppers
Turnip	Yams	Bok choy

VEGETABLES

Broccoli

Brussels sprouts

Cabbage (all varieties)

Carrots

Cauliflower

Celery

Celery root

Collard greens

Cucumbers

Edamame (soy beans)

Eggplant

Escarole

Fennel

Fiddleheads

Fresh herbs

Garlic

Gingerroot

Green onions

Horseradish

Kale

Kohlrabi

Leeks

Lettuce (all varieties)

VEGETABLES

Mushrooms (all varieties)

Mustard greens

New potatoes

Okra

Onions

Peas

Peppers (sweet or hot)

Radicchio

Radishes

Rapini

Shallots

Snow peas

Spinach

Sugar snap peas

Sun-dried tomatoes

Swiss chard

Tomatoes

Watercress

Zucchini

SOY FOODS

	Soy cheese	Soy cheese (low fat)
	Tofu	Tofu (low fat)
		Veggie breakfast links
		Veggie burgers
		Veggie ground round

FRESH FRUIT

Cantaloupe	Apricots	Apples
Honeydew melon	Bananas	Asian pears
Watermelon	Coconut	Avocado
	Custard apples	Blackberries
	Kiwi	Blueberries
	Mango	Cherries
	Papaya	Clementines
	Passion fruit	Cranberries
	Pineapple	Grapefruit
	Pomegranates	Grapes
		Guavas
		Lemons
		Mandarin oranges
		Nectarines
		Oranges
		Peaches

FRESH FRUIT

		Pears
		Plums
		Raspberries
		Rhubarb
		Strawberries
		Tangerines

NUTS

Chocolate-covered nuts	Brazil nuts	Almonds
	Peanuts	Cashews
	Pecans	Hazelnuts
	Walnuts	Macadamias
		Pistachios

DRIED FRUIT

Dates	Dried apricots	Dried apples
Dried mango	Dried cranberries	
Dried papaya	Prunes	
Dried pineapple		
Figs		
Raisins		

The Deli Counter

Most processed meats are high in fat, sodium and nitrates and are therefore red light. There are, however, a few yellow- and green-light options. Cheese, too, is pretty much a diet villain, since it's high in saturated fats. However, for flavour, it can be sprinkled sparingly on salads, omelettes and pasta.

PROCESSED MEAT		
Bologna	Corned beef	Chicken breast
Hot dogs		Lean ham
Kielbasa		Pastrami (turkey)
Liverwurst		
Pancetta		Turkey breast
Pastrami (beef)		Turkey roll
Pâté		
Roast beef		
Salami		
Sausage		
Smoked meat		

CHEESE		
Most cheese	Low-fat cheese	Extra low-fat cheese (e.g., Laughing Cow Light, Boursin Light)
		Fat-free cheese

BREAD		
Flatbread	Thin whole wheat pizza crust	Whole-grain, high-fibre breads (2.5–3 g fibre per slice)

OTHER		
Blue cheese dip	Baba ghanouj	Olives
Butternut squash dip		Hummus
Coleslaw		Roasted red pepper dip
Macaroni salad		
Polenta		
Tuna salad		
Tzatziki		

The Bakery

Anything that is made primarily of bleached white flour—which has one of the highest G.I. ratings of any food—is red light. Because most people are in the habit of eating white bread, which has been stripped of most of its nutrients, they are unused to whole-grain breads. But once you give them a chance, I think you'll find green-light breads far more flavourful than bland white loaves.

Always check labels when choosing a loaf. The first ingredient should be 100 percent whole wheat or whole-grain flour, and there should be a minimum of 2.5 to 3.0 grams of fibre per slice.

While all the desserts you'll find in the bakery section are red-light because of the white flour and sugar in them, you can make your own delectable desserts at home, using the recipes in *The G.I. Diet* and *Living the G.I. Diet.*

BREADS		
Bagels Baguette Bread crumbs Calabrese	Crispbreads (with fibre) Pita (whole wheat)	100% stone-ground whole wheat bread

BREADS

Crispbreads (regular)	Tortillas (whole wheat)	Crispbreads (with high fibre, e.g., Wasa Fibre)
Croissants	Whole-grain breads	
Croutons		Whole-grain, high-fibre breads (2.5 -3 g fibre per slice)
Crumpets		
English muffins		
Hamburger buns		
Hot dog buns		
Ice cream cones		
Kaiser rolls		
Muffins		
Pita		
Raisin bread		
Stuffing		
Tortillas		
White bread		

DESSERTS

Cake		
Cookies		
Danishes		
Donuts		
Pies		
Tarts		

The Fish Counter

All fish and shellfish are green light and provide a wide variety of wonderful meals. Some people are under the mistaken belief that oily fish, such as salmon and mackerel, isn't good for you. In fact, oily fish is rich in omega-3 and is therefore extremely beneficial for heart health.

FISH		
All breaded fish	Salt cod	All fresh fish
Fish canned in oil		All frozen fish
Sushi		Caviar
		Fish canned in water
		Pickled herring
		Sashimi
		Smoked fish

SHELLFISH

Breaded calamari	Seafood salads	Canned clams
Breaded clams		Canned crab
Breaded scallops		Canned lobster
Breaded shrimp		Canned shrimp
Seafood pâté		Fresh clams
		Fresh crab
		Imitation crab
		Lobster
		Mussels
		Oysters
		Scallops
		Shrimp
		Smoked oysters
		Squid

The Meat Counter

Meat always contains some fat, but some cuts have far less than others. Simply trimming visible fat can reduce the overall amount by an average of 50 percent. Remember to keep the serving size to 4 ounces, which is about the size of the palm of your hand.

Skinless chicken or turkey breast is really the benchmark for low-fat protein. Dark meat, or thighs and legs, duck and goose are higher in saturated fat.

BEEF		
Brisket	Beef jerky	Extra-lean ground beef
Regular ground beef	Corned beef	Eye round
Sausage	Lean ground beef	T-bone
Short ribs	Sirloin	Top round
	Sirloin tip	
	Tenderloin	

PORK		
Back ribs	Centre loin	Back bacon
Blade	Fresh ham	Lean deli ham
Regular bacon	Shank	Tenderloin
Sausage	Sirloin	
Spareribs	Top loin	

CHICKEN, CAPON AND TURKEY		
Breast with skin	Roasters/stewing light/dark without skin	Breast without skin
Roasters/stewing light/dark with skin	Thigh without skin	
Thigh with skin	Turkey bacon	
Wing with skin	Turkey sausage	

VEAL		
Breaded cutlets		Blade steak
Sausage		Cutlets
		Loin chop
		Rib roast
		Shank

LAMB		
Rack	Fore shank	
Sausage	Leg shank	
	Loin chop	

DUCK AND GOOSE		
Duck (all parts)		
Goose (all parts)		

OTHER		
Offal		Bison (Buffalo)
Organ Meat		Elk
		Emu
		Ostrich
		Rabbit
		Venison

The Beans (Legumes) and Canned Vegetables Aisle

Beans, or legumes, are the perfect green-light food. They are rich in protein and fibre and low in fat. Canned beans are more convenient than dried beans, but the canning process significantly raises their G.I. rating—sometimes up to 50 percent. Likewise with vegetables. It is always preferable to buy fresh or frozen vegetables rather than canned.

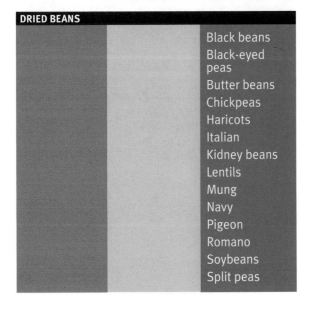

DRIED BEANS

Black beans
Black-eyed peas
Butter beans
Chickpeas
Haricots
Italian
Kidney beans
Lentils
Mung
Navy
Pigeon
Romano
Soybeans
Split peas

CANNED BEANS		
Baked beans with pork	Baked beans	Baked beans (low fat)
Broad	Chili	Black beans
Refried		Black-eyed peas
		Butter beans
		Chickpeas
		Haricots
		Italian
		Lentils
		Mung
		Navy
		Pigeon
		Romano
		Soybeans

CANNED AND BOTTLED VEGETABLES		
Artichoke hearts	Most canned vegetables	Canned tomatoes
Creamed corn	Sun-dried tomatoes in oil	Roasted red peppers
Beets		Tomato paste
Peas		
Potatoes		
Sweet potatoes		
Yams		

The Pasta and Sauces Aisle

Most pasta is green light, and whole wheat pasta is even more so. Make sure to always slightly under-cook pasta—until it's just *al dente,* as Italians say—and watch the serving size (¾ cup cooked per serving).

Choose low-sugar pasta sauces made primarily of tomatoes. Tomato sauce happens to be rich in lycoprene, which has been shown to reduce the risk of prostate cancer. Sauces with cream and/or cheese are, of course, red light.

PASTA		
All canned pasta	Rice noodles	Capellini
Gnocchi		Fettuccine
Macaroni and cheese		Linguine
Noodles (canned or instant)		Macaroni
		Penne
Pasta filled with cheese or meat		Rigatoni
		Spaghetti
		Vermicelli

PASTA SAUCES		
Alfredo	Basil pesto	Healthy Choice pasta sauces
Cream sauces	Sauces with vegetables (no added sugar)	Light sauces with vegetables (no added sugar)
Sauces with added meat or cheese	Sun-dried tomato pesto	
Sauces with added sugar or sucrose		Too Good To Be True pasta sauces

The Soup and Canned Seafood and Meat Aisle

Canned soups generally have a higher G.I. rating than soups made from scratch because of the high processing temperatures needed to prevent spoilage. So if you have the time, it's worthwhile to make your own with green-light ingredients. The best canned soups are the ones that are vegetable-based, are not puréed and don't contain cream.

SOUP		
All cream-based soups	Canned chicken noodle	Bouillon (low sodium)
Canned black bean	Canned lentil	Campbells' Healthy Request soups
Canned green pea	Canned tomato	Canned low-fat bean and vegetable soups
Canned puréed vegetable		
Canned split pea		Miso soup
Instant soups		Too Good To Be True soups

CANNED SEAFOOD

Fish canned in oil		Crab
		Fish canned in water
		Shrimp
		Smoked oysters

CANNED MEAT

Beef	Chicken	
Ham	Turkey	
Pork		
Spam		

The Grains and Side Dishes Aisle

Whole grains with all the nutrition and fibre intact are usually green light. With rice, it all depends on the variety, because some contain a starch, amylase, that breaks down slowly.

GRAINS		
Arborio rice	Cornmeal	Barley
Couscous	Kamut	Basmati rice
Grits	Kasha	Brown rice
Instant rice	Spelt	Buckwheat
Jasmine rice		Bulgur
Millet		Graham
Semolina		Flax seeds
Short-grain rice		Long-grain rice
Sticky rice		Quinoa
		Wheat berries
		Wild rice

SIDE DISHES		
Instant noodles		
Instant potatoes		
Stuffing		

The International Foods Aisle

ASIAN

Canned lychees in syrup	Black bean sauce	Buckwheat noodles
Chow mein noodles	Canned baby corn	Canned bamboo shoots
Chutney	Canned lychees in juice	Canned water chestnuts
Coconut milk	Chili-garlic sauce	Cellophane (mung bean) noodles
Ghee	Coconut milk (light)	Curry paste
Honey garlic sauce	Fish sauce	Dried seaweed
Instant noodles	Oyster sauce	Hoisin sauce
Plum sauce	Pappadums (baked)	Hot chili paste
Ramen noodles	Rice noodles	Miso
Sweet and sour sauce	Rice wine	Pickled ginger
	Sesame oil	Rice vinegar
	Soy sauce (regular)	Soy sauce (low sodium)
	Udon noodles	Teriyaki sauce
		Vermicelli
		Wasabi

MEXICAN		
Refried beans Taco shells Tortillas Tostadas	Salsa (with added sugar) Taco sauce (with added sugar)	Canned green chiles Chipotle en adobo Pickled jalapenos Salsa (with no added sugar) Taco sauce (with no added sugar)

MIDDLE EASTERN		
Couscous Pita bread Stuffed grape leaves	Baba ghanouj Whole wheat pita bread	Falafel mix Hummus Tahini

The Cooking Oil, Vinegar, Salad Dressing and Pickles Aisle

Choosing the right oil to use in cooking and on salads is critical to your heart health. Saturated and hydrogenated oils are dangerous and should be avoided. Canola and olive oils get the green light.

Because acid tends to reduce the G.I. rating of a meal—it slows the digestive process—vinegars and vinaigrettes are great additions. Dressings should always be low-fat, but be careful of sugar levels. Sometimes producers will raise the sugar level as they reduce the oil to improve flavour. Be sure to check labels and compare low-fat brands.

COOKING OIL		
Coconut oil	Corn oil	Canola oil
Palm oil	Peanut oil	Extra-virgin olive oil
Vegetable shortening	Sesame oil	Flax oil
	Soybean oil	Olive oil
	Sunflower oil	Vegetable oil spray
	Vegetable oil	

VINEGAR		
		Balsamic vinegar
		Cider vinegar
		Red wine vinegar
		Rice vinegar
		White vinegar
		White wine vinegar

SALAD DRESSINGS		
Regular salad dressings	Light salad dressings	Low-fat, low-sugar salad dressings
		Low-fat, low-sugar vinaigrettes

PICKLES		
Branston pickle	Sun-dried tomatoes in oil	Capers
Bread and butter pickles		Cocktail onions
Chow chow		Dill pickles
Chutney		Olives
Gherkins		Pickled hot peppers
Pickled beets		Pickled mixed vegetables
Sweet mustard pickles		Pickled mush-rooms
		Sauerkraut

CONDIMENTS		
Barbecue sauce	Hot sauce	Dijon mustard
Chili sauce	Salsa (with added sugar)	Gravy mix (maximum 20 calories per 1/4 cup serving)
Honey mustard		
Ketchup		
Mayonnaise		Horseradish
Relish		Mayonnaise (fat free)
Steak sauce		
Tartar sauce		Mustard
		Salsa (no added sugar)
		Seafood cocktail sauce
		Tabasco
		Worcestershire sauce

The Snacks Aisle

Unfortunately, the snacks aisle at the supermarket is full of red-light temptation. Still, all you G.I. Dieters need three snacks a day—green-light ones of course. If you purchase food bars, make sure they contain 20 to 30 grams of carbohydrates, 12 to 15 grams of protein and 5 grams of fat. Good green-light choices are Balance and Zone bars (half a bar per serving).

SNACKS		
Candy	Crispbreads (with fibre)	Almonds
Caramel-coated popcorn	Dark chocolate (70% cocoa)	Applesauce (unsweetened)
Cheesies	Most nuts	Canned fruit salad
Cookies	Popcorn (air-popped)	Canned mandarin oranges
Crackers	Roasted peanuts	Canned peaches in juice or water
Crispbreads (regular)	Salsa (with added sugar)	Canned pears in juice or water
Flavoured gelatin (all varieties)		Cashews
Fruit leather		
Granola bars		
Ice cream cones		

SNACKS		
Melba toast		Crispbreads with high fibre, e.g., Wasa Fibre)
Party mix		
Popcorn (regular)		Food bars
Potato chips		Fruit bowls with no added sugar
Pretzels		Hazelnuts
Pudding		Macadamia nuts
Rice cakes		
Rice chips		Pistachios
Rice crackers		Pumpkin seeds
Tortilla chips		Salsa (with no added sugar)
Trail mix		Soynuts
		Sugar-free hard candies
		Sunflower seeds

The Baking Aisle

Though you can't eat ready-made baked goods from the supermarket when you're trying to lose weight, you can bake your own sweet treats using recipes from *The G.I. Diet* and *Living the G.I. Diet.* They call for sugar substitutes rather than sugar, honey or molasses. Our favourite brand of sweetener is Splenda, which is derived from sugar but doesn't have the calories. It measures by volume exactly as sugar does. Although dried fruit such as raisins and cranberries are red- and yellow-light, small amounts are acceptable for baking.

SWEETENERS		
Corn syrup	Fructose	Aspartame
Glucose		Brown sugar substitute (e.g., Sugar Twin)
Honey		
Molasses		Equal
Sugar (all types)		Splenda
		Stevia (note: not FDA approved)
		Sugar Twin
		Sweet'N Low

BAKING SUPPLIES

Cake mixes

Canned cranberry sauce

Canned pumpkin

Chocolate chips

Cookie mixes

Evaporated milk

Glacé cherries

Graham cracker crumbs

Icing

Lard

Maraschino cherries

Mincemeat

Muffin mixes

Peanut butter (regular and light)

Pie filling

Raisins

Sweetened condensed milk

Vegetable shortening

White flour

Baking chocolate (unsweetened)

Coconut

Dried apricots

Dried cranberries

Natural nut butters

Natural peanut butter

Peanuts

Pecans

Pine nuts

Prunes

Walnuts

Almonds

Baking powder

Baking soda

Cashews

Cocoa

Hazelnuts

Macadamia nuts

Oat bran

Pumpkin seeds

Sunflower seeds

Wheat bran

Wheat germ

Whole wheat flour

SPICES AND FLAVOURINGS

Coating for poultry or pork	Bouillon Bovril Marmite	Bouillon (low sodium) Dried herbs Extracts (vanilla, etc.) Gravy mixes (20 calories maximum per 1/4 cup serving) Lemon juice Lime juice Pepper Salt Seasoning mixes with no added sugar Spices

The Breakfast Foods Aisle

Of course, the king of breakfast foods is old-fashioned oatmeal—the large-flake kind, not instant or quick oats. Most cereals on the market are red light. They are made from highly processed grains that lack both nutrition and fibre. Beware of those so-called healthy or natural granola types of cereal, because they, too, are usually low in fibre and high in sugar. What you should be looking for are cereals that have at least 10 grams of fibre per serving. While they may not seem much fun in themselves, they can be dressed up with nuts, fruit and yogurt. Cereal bars are absolutely red light—they're full of sugar. Better to go for a Balance or Zone bar or equivalent.

While packaged pancake mixes and frozen waffles are red light, you can make green-light versions yourself (the recipes are in *Living the G.I. Diet).* Low-sugar fruit spreads that list fruit as the first ingredient are wonderful green-light additions to toast, cereal and low-fat dairy products such as yogurt and cottage cheese.

CEREAL

All cold cereals except those listed as yellow or red light	Kashi Go Lean Crunch	100% Bran
Cereal bars	Kashi Good Friends	All-Bran
Cream of wheat	Red River	Bran Buds
Granola	Shredded Wheat Bran	Fibre 1
Instant porridge		Fibre First
Muesli		Kashi Go Lean
Quick-cooking oatmeal		Large-flake oatmeal
		Oat bran
		Steel-cut Irish oatmeal

PANCAKES AND SYRUPS

Corn syrup		
Maple syrup		
Molasses		
Pancake mix		
Pancake syrup		

SPREADS

Fruit spreads (regular)	Natural nut butters	Fruit spreads (extra fruit, no added sugar)
Jam	Natural peanut butter	
Marmalade		
Nutella		
Peanut butter (regular and light)		

The Beverage Aisle

You need up to eight glasses of liquid a day to keep your body hydrated and healthy. Drinks with caffeine tend to stimulate the appetite and so are red light. The exception is tea, which has far less caffeine than either coffee or soft drinks. Juice is not worth the calories—eat the fruit instead. In addition to the green-light beverages listed below, remember that skim milk and light plain soy milk, which are found in the dairy section, also make refreshing and nutritious drinks.

BEVERAGES		
Chocolate milk mix	Diet soft drinks (caffeinated)	Bottled water (carbonated or non-carbonated)
Coffee whitener	Most unsweetened juice	Club soda
Evaporated milk	Non-alcoholic beer	Decaffeinated coffee
Fruit crystals	Vegetable juices	Diet soft drinks (without caffeine)
Fruit drinks		Herbal teas
Hot chocolate (regular)		Hot chocolate (light)
Regular coffee		

BEVERAGES

Regular iced tea		Iced tea (with no added sugar)
Regular soft drinks		Tea (with or without caffeine)
Sports drinks		
Sweetened condensed milk		
Sweetened juice		
Watermelon juice		

The Dairy Case

Low-fat dairy products are a G.I. Diet staple. They are rich in protein, calcium and vitamin D. Regular dairy products contain a high amount of saturated fat and are therefore red light. But you can lightly sprinkle full-flavoured cheeses such as old cheddar, feta and Parmesan over salads, omelettes and pasta. If you are lactose intolerant, low-fat soy products are an excellent alternative—just make sure they aren't laden with sugar.

There is a wide selection of non-dairy products in the dairy case, such as pickles, cookie dough and anchovy paste. I've listed some of these items too.

MILK		
Almond milk	1% milk	Buttermilk
Chocolate milk		Skim milk
Cream		Soy milk (plain, low-fat)
Goat milk		
Regular soy milk		
Rice milk		
Whole or 2% milk		

CHEESE		
Cheese (regular)	Cheese (low-fat)	Cheese (fat-free)
Cheese spread	Low-fat cream cheese	Cottage cheese (1% or fat-free)
Cottage cheese (whole or 2%)	Low-fat string cheese	Extra low-fat cheese (e.g., Laughing Cow Light, Boursin Light)
Cream cheese	Regular soy cheese	
		Low-fat soy cheese

YOGURT AND SOUR CREAM		
Sour cream	Sour cream (light)	Fruit yogurt (nonfat with sugar substitute)
Yogurt (whole or 2%)	Yogurt (low-fat with sugar)	
		Sour cream (nonfat)

BUTTER AND MARGARINE		
Butter	Soft margarine (nonhydrogenated)	Soft margarine (nonhydrogenated, light)
Hard margarine		

EGGS		
Whole regular eggs	Whole omega-3 eggs	Egg whites in cartons
		Liquid eggs in cartons
		Naturegg Break Free
		Naturegg Omega Pro

OTHER		
Bread and butter pickles	Anchovy paste	Dill pickles
Eggnog	Unsweetened juice	Gefilte fish
Cookie dough		Horseradish
Dips		Pickled herring
Flavoured gelatin		Pickled sweet pimentos
Pickled eggs		Pickled tomatoes
Pudding		
Sweetened juice		

The Frozen Food Section

Almost all of the prepared meals you find in the frozen food section of your grocery store are red light because of the ingredients used and the way in which they've been processed. Still, the freezer section is a great source for green-light convenience foods such as frozen vegetables and fruit, fish and green-light desserts. Make sure the vegetables aren't in a butter, cream or cheese sauce—that's definitely red light!

VEGETABLES		
Broad beans	Artichoke hearts	Asparagus
French fries	Corn	Beans (green/wax)
Hash browns	Squash	Bell peppers
Lima beans		Broccoli
Rutabaga		Brussels sprouts
Vegetables in a butter, cream or cheese sauce		Carrots
		Cauliflower
		Fiddleheads
		Okra
		Peas
		Spinach

PREPARED FOOD

Appetizers	Lean burgers	Chicken souvlaki
Chicken wings	Pork souvlaki	Extra-lean burgers
Dumplings	Turkey burgers	
Lasagna		Frozen fish without breaded coating
Meat pies		
Pasta filled with cheese or meat		Scallops without breaded coating
Perogies		
Pizza		Shrimp without breaded coating
Rice dishes		
TV dinners		Veggie burgers
White bread		Veggie ground round

BREAKFAST

Hash browns		Egg Beaters
Sausages		Veggie breakfast links
Waffles		

DESSERTS		
Frozen soy desserts (regular)	Fruit bars (no added sugar)	Breyers Smart Scoop Fat Free Frozen Dessert
Ice cream (regular)		Frozen soy desserts with about 100 calories or less per 1/2 cup
Pie		
Pie and tart shells		
Popsicles		Ice cream (low-fat and no added sugar)
Puff pastry		
Tartufo		Nestlé's Legend No Added Sugar ice cream
Whipped topping		

FRUIT		
		Blackberries
		Blueberries
		Cherries
		Cranberries
		Peaches
		Raspberries
		Rhubarb
		Strawberries

PART TWO

Eating Out

Fast Food

Just a few years ago, the idea of ordering a green-light lunch at a fast food outlet was simply laughable—but no longer! Due in part to the threat of legal action and in part to stagnant market shares, the major fast food chains are finally offering some healthy options. In all fairness, Subway has been pioneering the move toward fast, healthy meals for some time now, and their initiative has been reflected in their phenomenal growth. They have actually replaced McDonald's as North America's number one fast food chain.

Unfortunately, the majority of the food on offer at fast food restaurants is still red light: hamburgers soaked in saturated fat, fish and chicken coated in deep-fried batter, and all the trimmings, such as fries, sodas, shakes and ketchup, loaded with fat and sugar. To compound this dietary disaster, you can supersize everything! No wonder we're setting obesity records and becoming diabetics at an exponential rate.

So, what are the points of light in this sea of gloom? I've listed them by each major fast food chain. Remember to always throw away the top half of the bun on burgers or sandwiches and eat them open-faced; and to ask for low-fat dressings and use only half the packet on your salad.

One of the health issues that is rarely mentioned in the debate on fast food is sodium levels. When creating lower fat products, the fast food industry frequently boosts salt content to make up for any perceived flavour shortfall. The problem is that sodium increases water retention, which causes bloating and extra weight—especially in women—and raises blood pressure. The official recommended daily allowance of sodium is 2,500 milligrams, but many authorities are calling for a reduction to 1,500 milligrams. On average we consume three times that. Though Swiss Chalet's Grilled Chicken Breast on Rice appears to be a healthy, low-fat meal, it contains 2,420 milligrams of sodium, or nearly twice what you need for an entire day! In order to alert you to the sodium levels in the fast food I've listed, I've asterixed those items that have excessively high levels, and double-asterixed the ones that reach a stratospheric level.

McDonald's

Salads

Chicken Oriental Salad

Dressings

Newman's Own Low Fat Balsamic*

Newman's Own Low Fat Sesame Thai*

Burgers

Whole Wheat Chicken McGrill with BBQ sauce*

Chicken Protein Platter*

Snack

Fruit 'n Yogurt Parfait (hold the granola)

Wendy's

Salads
Mandarin Chicken Salad
Spring Mix Salad

Dressings
Fat Free French Style
Reduced Fat Creamy Ranch
Low Fat Honey Mustard

Burgers
Ultimate Chicken Grill* plus side salad

Chili
Large chili plus side salad

Snack
Jr. Frosty Dairy Dessert (6 oz cup)

Burger King

Remember to hold the Parmesan toast on all salads.

Salads
Fire-Grilled Chicken or Shrimp Caesar Salad
Fire-Grilled Chicken or Shrimp Garden Salad

Dressings
Fat-Free Honey Mustard
Hidden Valley Fat-Free Ranch

Burgers
BK VEGGIE* plus side salad

Harvey's

Salads
Entrée Grilled Chicken Caesar Salad
Entrée Grilled Chicken Garden Salad
Entrée Caesar Salad

Dressings
Light Caesar
Light Italian

Soups
Beef Barley*
Chicken Noodle*
Harvest Vegetable*

Burgers
Signature Grilled Chicken*
Veggieburger

Subway

The best choice of roll for a sub is Italian or Wheat.

Subs (6-inch)
Roast Beef*
Oven Roasted Chicken Breast
Savory Turkey Breast*
Turkey Breast, Ham and Roast Beef*
Veggie Delite
Sweet Onion Chicken Teriyaki*
Ham*

Deli-Style Sandwiches
Ham
Roast Beef
Savory Turkey Breast

Salads
Garden Fresh (side salad)
Mediterranean Chicken

Dressings
Honey Mustard Sauce
Red Wine Vinaigrette
Sweet Onion Sauce

Tim Hortons

Ask that your sandwich be made with a whole wheat bun.

Sandwiches

Garden Vegetable

Harvest Turkey Breast

Albacore Tuna Salad*

Turkey Bacon Club**

Chicken and Roasted Red Pepper*

Soups

"Tim's Own" chicken noodle*

Vegetable beef barley*

Hearty vegetable*

Turkey and rice*

Beef noodle*

Chicken gumbo*

Tomato florentine*

Minestrone*

Chili

Chili

Swiss Chalet

Always hold the flatbread on the following meals.

Meals
Santa Fe Grilled Chicken Salad**
Vegetable Stir Fry on rice*
Chicken Stir Fry on rice**
Quarter Chicken White (skinless) with
    coleslaw/vegetables/corn
Chicken on a Kaiser (eat open-faced)

Dressings
Light Italian
Fat-Free Raspberry Vinaigrette

Note: This information was correct when this guide went to press. However, as this is a dynamic field, you may wish to check the websites of fast food chains from time to time to see if they have expanded their green-light offerings.

Restaurants

It isn't difficult to dine out the green-light way now that restaurants are following healthy trends such as broiling and grilling instead of frying, using vegetable oils and offering a greater variety of fish dishes, vegetables and salads. Here are my top ten tips for ensuring your night out doesn't leave you feeling guilty the next day:

1. Eat a small bowl of green-light cereal with skim milk and sweetener just before you leave for the restaurant. This will give you some extra fibre and help take the edge off your appetite.

2. On arrival at the restaurant, drink a glass of water to help you feel a bit fuller. Feel free to

enjoy a glass of red wine, but wait until the main course arrives to drink it.

3. Once the habitual basket of rolls or bread—which you ignore—has been passed around the table, ask the waiter to remove it. The longer it sits there, the more tempted you'll be to dig in.

4. Order a chunky vegetable-based soup or a salad with the dressing on the side (no Caesar) to start with, and tell your waiter you'd like this as soon as possible.

5. Ask for vegetables instead of potatoes and rice, since you can't be sure what type will be served.

6. Stick with low-fat cuts of meat or poultry (see page 22–23), or choose fish or shellfish that isn't breaded or battered. Because restaurant servings tend to be overly generous, remember to eat only 4 to 6 ounces (about the size of a pack of cards) and leave the rest.

7. Ask that any sauces that come with your meal be put on the side.

8. Desserts are almost always a dietary minefield with not a lot of green-light choices. Fresh fruit or berries without ice cream is the best option. Or perhaps order a decaffeinated skim-milk latte and sweeten it with sugar substitute.

   If social pressure to have a rich dessert becomes overwhelming, ask for extra forks so it can be shared. A couple of forkfuls or so with your coffee should get you off the hook with minimal dietary damage!

9. Order only decaffeinated coffee or tea. My favourite choice is a nonfat decaf cappuccino.

10. Finally, and perhaps most importantly, **eat slowly**. The famous Dr. Johnson advised chewing food thirty-two times before swallowing! Although that is a bit over the top, at least try to put your fork down between mouthfuls. The stomach can take between 20 and 30 minutes to let the brain know it's full.

All-You-Can-Eat Buffets

A buffet can be your best or worst option, depending on your level of self-control. While you're free to make your own selections, there may be a lot of red-light temptations there. I suggest you do a quick reconnaissance of the whole buffet before picking up your plate and starting in. This will ensure there's still space on your plate when you reach your favourite foods. Follow the G.I. Diet ground rules, and the buffet will be your best dining-out option bar none.

International Cuisine

When eating the same type of food week after week starts to get a bit uninspiring, how about trying something completely new? I love international cuisine, particularly Italian, Greek, Chinese and Indian food. Because we're often unfamiliar with how an exotic dish is made, it's hard to determine whether it's green light or not. In this section I've tried to eliminate some of the guesswork by listing the dishes you'd typically find on a menu. Don't hesitate to ask your server about any dish I haven't mentioned. Here's a list of possible questions that could help give your meal a green light:

- Is this food fried, grilled or steamed?

- Could you ask the chef to prepare this dish without the cream sauce?

- Could the chef prepare this dish with the least amount of oil possible?

- Could I order only a half serving of this dish?

- Could you replace the potatoes with extra vegetables?

- Could I have the dressing/gravy/sauce on the side?

Italian

If you're serious about sticking to the G.I. Diet, it's really not a good idea to head to a pizzeria. Instead, go to a restaurant that has a wide variety of dishes on the menu. Usually these are divided into a number of parts: *L'antipasto,* which translates as "before the meal," includes hot and cold appetizers; *il primo,* or "the first course," includes pasta, pizza or risotto; *il secondo,* "the second course," includes meat, poultry or fish; and *il dolce* is "dessert."

Your best bets on the list of *antipasti* are soups containing beans and vegetables, such as minestrone, and salads, particularly the basic *insalata mista.* Remember to ask for the dressing on the side. Mussels are a good choice provided they are not served in a cream sauce. Other *antipasto* items such as roasted red peppers or mushrooms sound both delicious and healthy, but be careful of any that are marinated in oil. Although olive oil is beneficial, it is still calorie-dense. One cup equals the total daily calorie requirement for most people.

Although you should never make a meal of pasta, you can enjoy it as a first course. Choose pasta with a tomato-based sauce and share it with a dinner companion. Your serving should not exceed one quarter of the plate. Avoid pasta stuffed with meat and cheese, pasta in cream sauces and gnocchi. Decline the offer of grated cheese.

If you're craving pizza instead of pasta, choose one with a very thin crust, tomato sauce and vegetable toppings. Ask for no cheese except for a sprinkling of Parmesan. Then have only one slice, sharing the rest with the others at the table. Pizza should also be treated as an appetizer rather than as a meal.

For your *secondo,* choose grilled, roasted or braised fish, chicken or meat. Veal, a mainstay on Italian menus, is low in saturated fat and therefore an excellent choice, unless it is cooked in butter or served with cream sauce. Watch the serving size—you can always leave some on your plate if necessary. The Italian restaurant I frequent serves a fabulous veal chop, but it is about 14 ounces and comes with mashed potatoes. I ask for extra vegetables instead of the potatoes and share the veal with my wife, Ruth. We also order an extra vegetable or pasta dish to share.

For dessert I highly recommend a skim-milk decaf cappuccino—delicious! You won't miss the highly fattening tiramisu. If you're in a celebratory mood, treat yourself to some gelato, but since it is high in sugar, split it with a friend.

ITALIAN		
Breaded eggplant (or any breaded vegetable)	Mussels in wine sauce (no cream)	Grilled fish and chicken
Fried calamari	Roasted or braised lamb (loin/leg)	Grilled shrimp, scallops or calamari
Garlic bread	Thin-crust pizzas without cheese	Grilled, steamed or boiled vegetables
Gnocchi		
Mozzarella or bocconcini and tomato salads		
Pasta filled with meat or cheese		Mussels with tomato sauce (no wine)
Pasta with cream or cheese sauce		Pasta with seafood in tomato sauce (1/4 plate only)
Risotto		Pasta with vegetables in tomato sauce (1/4 plate only)
Salads with creamy dressings such as Caesar		Roasted fish
		Veal without cream or butter sauce

Greek

Greek restaurants often offer a selection of small dishes called meze. Two or three of these, such as hummus and grilled calamari can be a meal in themselves when served with small pieces of whole wheat pita and raw vegetables for dipping.

Grilled or baked seafood makes an excellent dinner choice. And the classic chicken souvlaki dinner can also be good. Though the serving sizes are often too large, just stick to the recommended green-light servings and you'll be fine. If the rice appears glutinous or sticky avoid it. If potatoes are served with the rice, ask for vegetables instead. A Greek salad often comes with your souvlaki dinner. If this is the case, ask that the feta and dressing be served on the side.

Greek desserts are calorie-laden—particularly the ever-popular baklava—and thus red light.

GREEK

Baklava	Baba ghanouj	Chicken souvlaki
Breaded calamari	Grilled lamb chops	Grilled or baked seafood
Dolmades	Grilled loin lamb chops	Hummus
Gyros	Lamb souvlaki	Melitzanosalata
Kleftiko	Pork souvlaki	
Moussaka	Vegetable gemistes	
Pastitsio		
Potato gemistes		
Spanakopita (spinach pie)		
Tzatziki		

Chinese

It's a real challenge to eat the green-light way at a Chinese restaurant. Much of the food is deep-fried or drowning in sweet sauces and therefore a disaster for your waistline. The sodium levels in the sauces are often very high, and saturated and trans fat oils are sometimes used in cooking. However it is not impossible to get a green-light meal. Pass on the spring rolls, crispy fried duck, fried rice and dumplings, and look for dishes that contain steamed or stir-fried vegetables with oyster sauce, garlic and ginger. Since many Chinese dishes rest on beds of rice or noodles, you need to pay attention to both type and amount. Most of the rice used is short grain with a glutinous sticky surface, and this is red light. Ask if they have long grain or brown rice instead—you may be lucky. Make sure it is steamed.

Noodles, for the most part, are red light, except for "cellophane noodles," which are made from mung beans. Keep the noodle proportion to no more than one quarter of your plate—it's too easy to heap them up. Stick with savoury sauces and avoid sweet and sour dishes. Try eating with chopsticks—they will slow you down so you end up eating less.

CHINESE

Chinese omelettes	Beef in black bean sauce	Cellophane noodles (mung bean noodles)
Chow mein	Egg noodles	Hot and sour soup
Dumplings	Stir-fried seafood, chicken or meat with vegetables (cooked in a small amount of oil)	Sautéed vegetables with garlic
Lo mein		Steamed seafood
Spring rolls		Steamed tofu with vegetables
Sweet and sour dishes		Steamed vegetables
Wonton soup		

Indian /South Asian

Vegetables, legumes and basmati rice are predominant in Indian cuisine. Many South Asians are vegetarians whose protein source is lentils and beans. Servings of meat, poultry or fish tend to be modest when used, and all this makes an Indian restaurant an excellent green-light dining option.

There are, however a few problems to watch for. The first is that the food is often fried. To make things worse, the food is often fried in "ghee," or clarified butter, a highly saturated fat. Be sure to ask your server how the food is prepared. Choose dishes that are baked or broiled.

The second problem is that full-fat dairy products are sometimes used. Try to avoid dishes with creamy sauces. And avoid the bread, which is often made with ghee. If you really, really want bread, choose baked whole wheat chapati. But it is better to have basmati rice instead. Don't have both.

Many restaurants offer their patrons heaped dishes of coconut slices, raisins and other sweeteners. These are red light. Similarly be careful of the addition of mangoes and papayas, which are yellow light, in dishes. Guavas are green light.

INDIAN

Butter chicken	Baked chapati	Balti vegetables
Chicken biryani	Prawns madras	Bengan bharta
Chicken korma		Chicken or fish saag
Chicken tikka masala		Chicken tikka
Curries with cream sauces		Chicken tikka kebab
Lamb rogan josh		Chicken vindaloo
Naan		Dal
Pakoras		Fish kebab
		Grilled fish
		Lentil or bean dishes without cream sauces
		Steamed basmati rice
		Tandoori chicken or fish
		Vegetable curries without cream sauces

Mexican/Latin American

Tex-Mex dishes that are heavy on cheese, refried beans, sour cream and tortillas are unsurprisingly red light. Most "blackened" dishes are pan-fried in garlic butter, and so must be avoided as well. Look for grilled seafood, chicken or meat with salsa, or dishes made with beans (not refried). Gazpacho soups made with tomatoes and peppers are excellent, as is ceviche, which is a seafood dish prepared with citrus juices.

MEXICAN		
Burritos	Chicken fajitas without the cheese and sour cream	Arroz a banda (fish with rice)
Chorizo		Baked fish
Nachos		Bean and vegetable soups
Quesadillas	Chicken or vegetable enchiladas with red sauce or salsa	Ceviche
		Chili with beans
	Chili with meat and beans	Chili with chicken and beans
		Gazpacho
		Grilled fish

Thai

Green-light eating is a challenge in Thai restaurants. In North America they tend to rely on sauces to create flavour, rather than spices and herbs as they do in Thailand. Many sauces are very sweet: tamarind sauce, Thai basil sauce and oyster sauce are all red light. Pad Thai, probably the most popular dish, is made with tamarind sauce and rice noodles. Curry sauces and peanut sauce are usually made with full-fat coconut milk and should be avoided, too. "Gee," you must be thinking, "is there anything I *can* eat in a Thai restaurant?"

The answer is yes. Start with a lemongrass soup (without coconut milk!) or mussels in a lemongrass broth. Then have a Thai beef salad, or a stir-fry with chicken and vegetables. Many Thai stir-fries are cooked quickly in small amounts of oil. Satays are also an excellent choice, but skip the peanut sauce. Have your satay with stir-fried or steamed vegetables and a green mango or papaya salad for a fabulous meal.

THAI

Curries containing coconut milk	Cold rolls (watch the dips)	Chicken or beef satays
Fried rice noodles	Green mango salad (dressing on the side)	Hot and sour soup
Fried spring rolls	Papaya salad	Seafood or vegetable soup without coconut milk
Pad Thai		Steamed seafood
Soups containing coconut milk		Thai beef or chicken salad (dressing on the side)
		Vegetables stir-fried with little oil

Japanese

There are lots of wonderful green-light options at Japanese restaurants once you get beyond the sushi and tempura. Sushi is red light because of the glutinous rice it is made with. Order sashimi instead, which is the fish without the rice. Watch the quantity of soy sauce you use—it's very high in sodium and should be thought of as liquid salt. Other Japanese specialties include wonderful soups made with clear broth bases, sukiyaki, which is a beef and vegetable stir-fry that uses a minimal amount of vegetable oil, and grilled fish. In many restaurants you can prepare your meal yourself in your own group pot. Nabemono is like a healthy fondue. Into the pot of boiling broth go chunks of vegetables, seafood and so on. Not only is it delicious, but it's a fun experience to share with friends. Miso soup is an excellent source of protein, and in Japan it is eaten at the end of the meal to aid digestion.

JAPANESE

Agemono (deep-fried)

Beef teriyaki

Deep-fried pork dishes

Gyoza (fried dumplings)

Oyako-donburi (chicken omelette over rice)

Sushi

Tempura

Chicken teriyaki

Noodle soups

Pickled salads

Shabu-shabu

Udon

Grilled seafood

Miso soup

Nabemono (seafood and vegetables in a broth)

Sashimi

Soba

Steamed rice and vegetables

Stir-fried vegetables

Sukiyaki

Sumashi wan (clear soup with tofu and shrimp)

Yosenabe (casseroles)

Index